This book belongs to

_____

Copyright © 2020 Inna Perelmuter
All rights reserved
No part of this publication may be reproduced, stored in a retrieval system or transmitted
in any form or by any means, electronic, mechanical, photocopying, recording or otherwise,
Without prior written permission from the author.

If you and your child enjoy this book, please give us a feedback at
www.amazon.com/author/inna.perelmuter

Now it is your turn!

Now it is your turn!

BIRD

1. Draw a circle for a head.

2. Draw a egg like shape a body.

3. Add small circle for an eye.

4. Add beak.

5. Add oval and lines for a wing.

6. Draw legs.

7. Draw ovals and lines for a tail.

8. Erase unwanted lines and color the bird.

Now it is your turn!

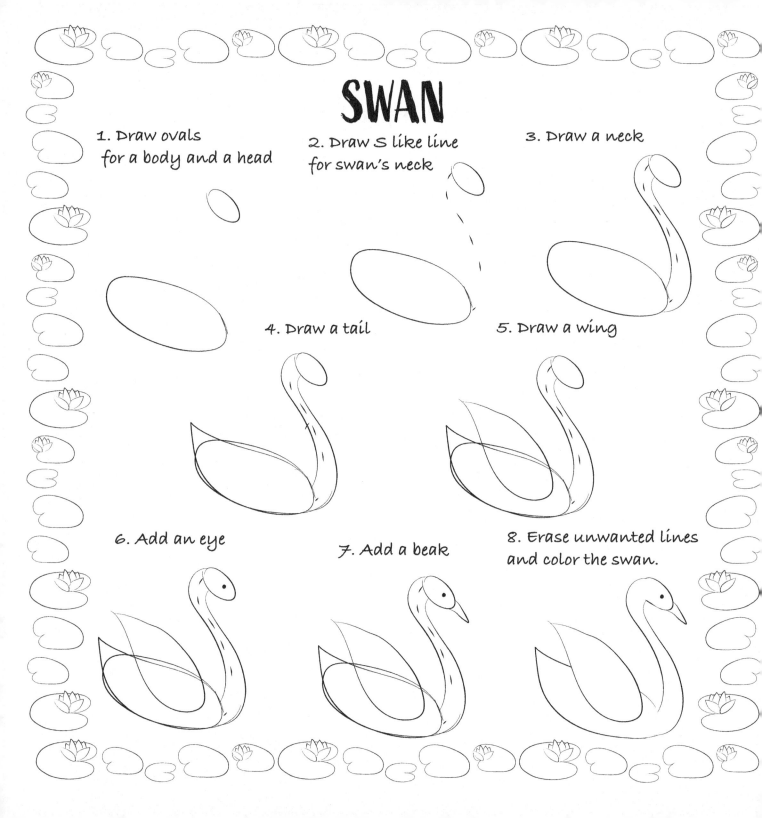

Now it is your turn!

HEDGEHOG

1. Draw an oval for a body and a head

2. Draw a curve for a nose

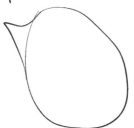

3. Draw a curve for a ear

4. Draw circles for a nose and a eye

5. Draw a vertical curve line

6. Draw arms and a legs

7. Draw zig-zag lanes to show quills

8. Erase unwanted lines and color the hedgehog.

Now it is your turn!

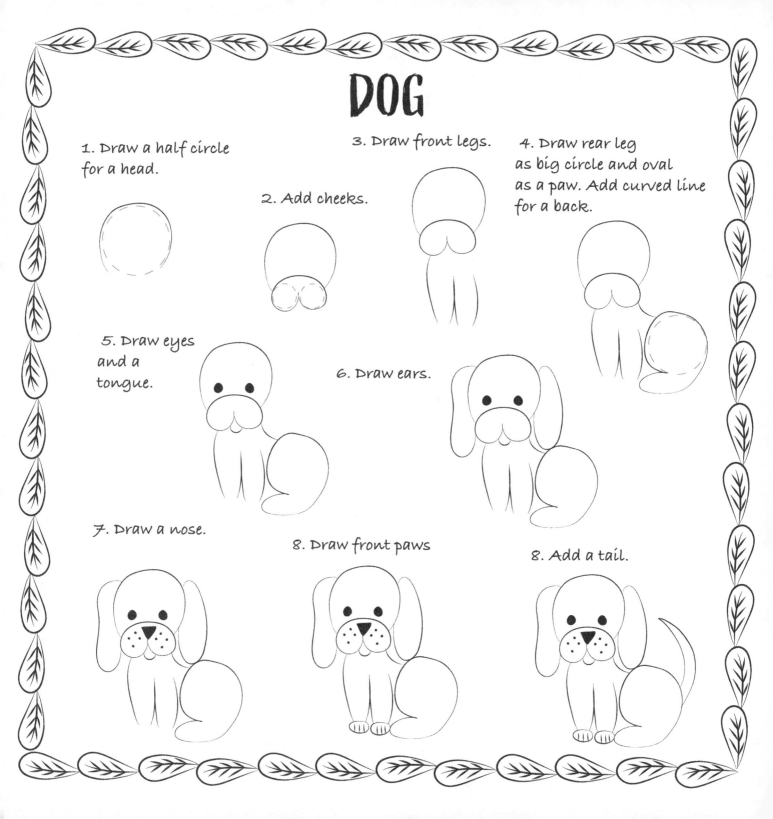

Now it is your turn!

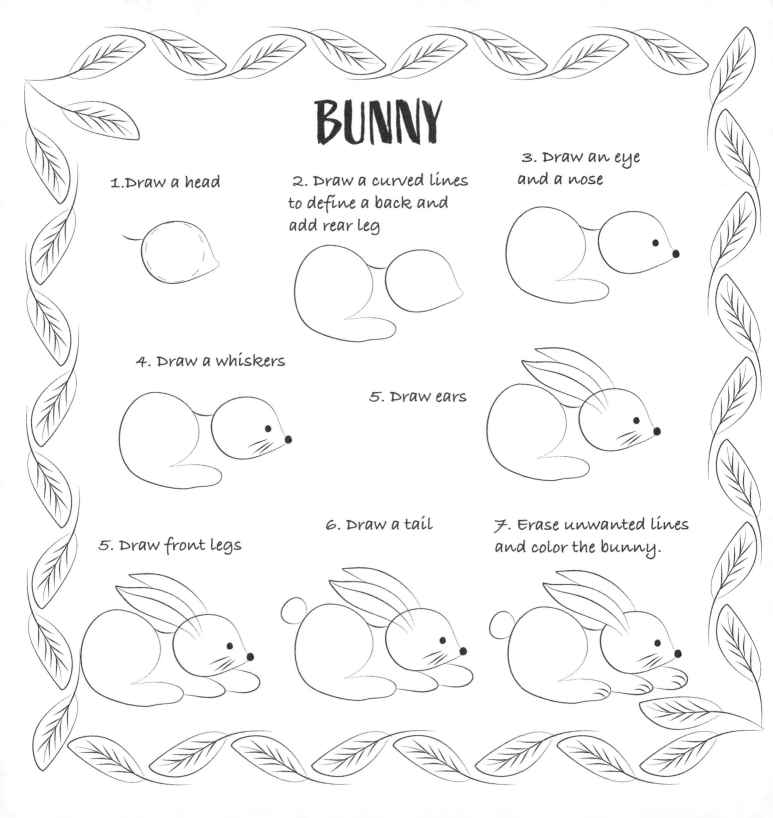

Now it is your turn!

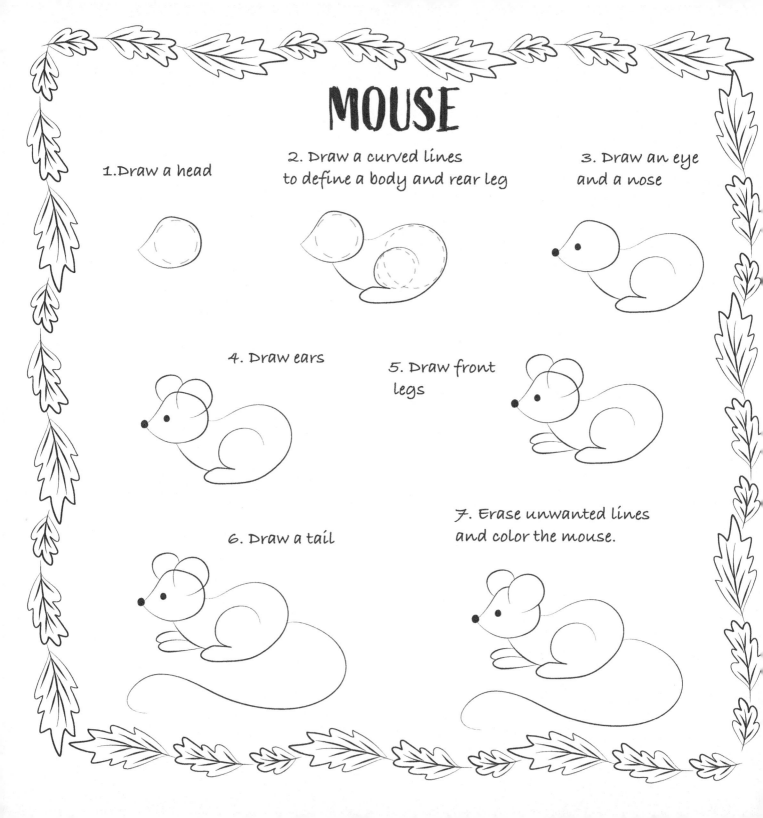

Now it is your turn!

Now it is your turn!

SEA STAR

1. Draw five lines from the center of the star
2. Draw an arms of the star
3. Erase lines in the middle.
4. Add curve for a smile
5. Add circles for eyes and smaller circles for pupils.
6. Draw small circles on the arms
7. Color the sea star if you wish

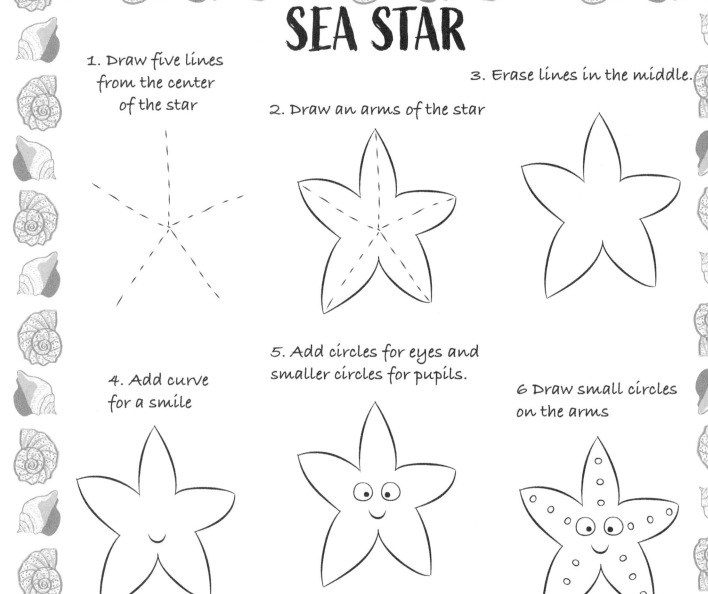

Now it is your turn!

SEA MOLLUSK

1. Draw a lower part of the shell

2. Draw a curve above it

3. Draw a few more on top of each other.

4. Draw a curve under the shell

5. Draw a curve for a mouth

6. Draw eyes and color the mollusk

Now it is your turn!

Now it is your turn!

WHALE

1. Draw a head and a body
2. Draw a curves to define a belly
3. Draw curves on the belly
4. Draw a fluke
5. Draw an eye
6. Draw a flipper
7. Erase unwanted lines and color the whale.

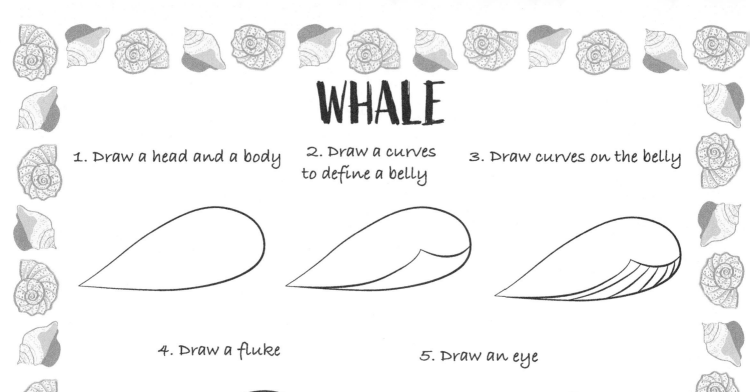

Now it is your turn!

Now it is your turn!

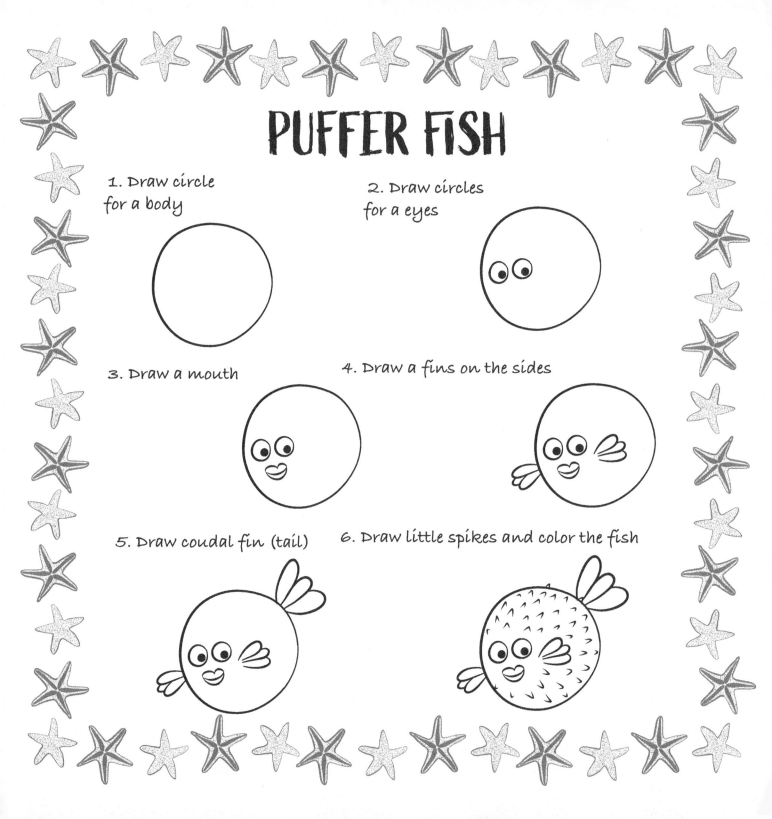

Now it is your turn!

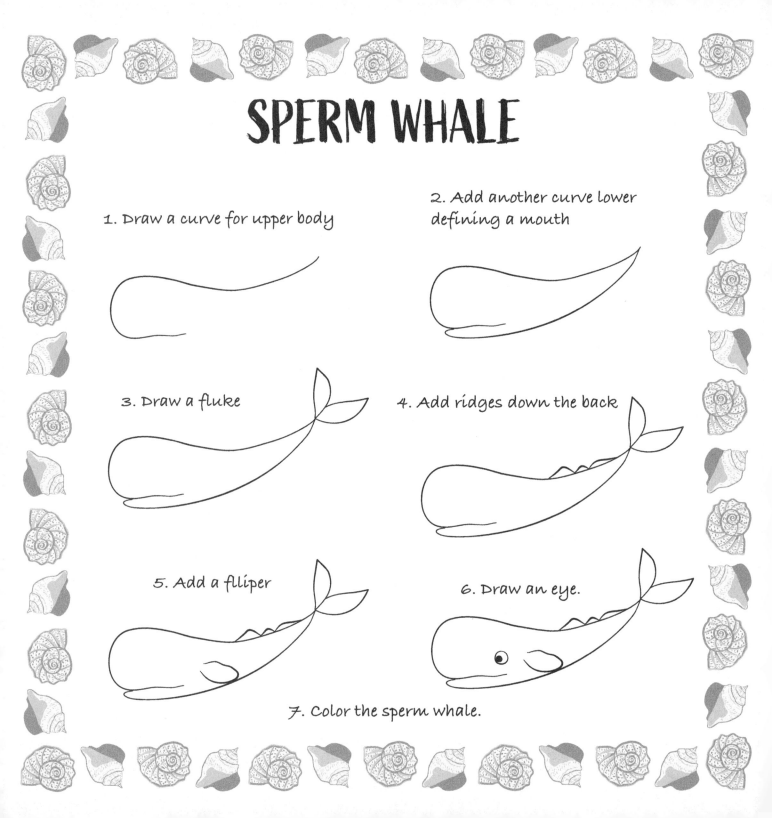

Now it is your turn!

FISH

1. Draw two curves for a body

2. Draw a curve to define a head

3. Draw caudal fin (tail)

4. Draw lips

5. Draw fins on the back and belly

6. Draw a fin on the side

7. Draw circle for an eye and curve for a gill

8. Draw details on the fin

9. Add scales and color the fish.

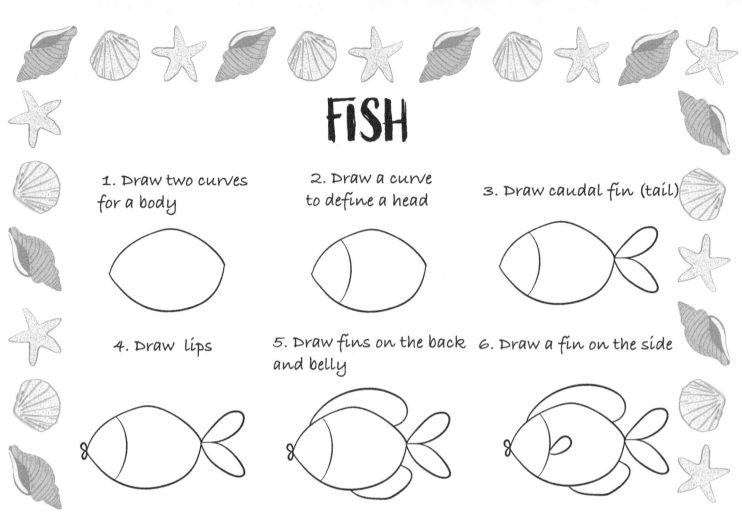

Now it is your turn!

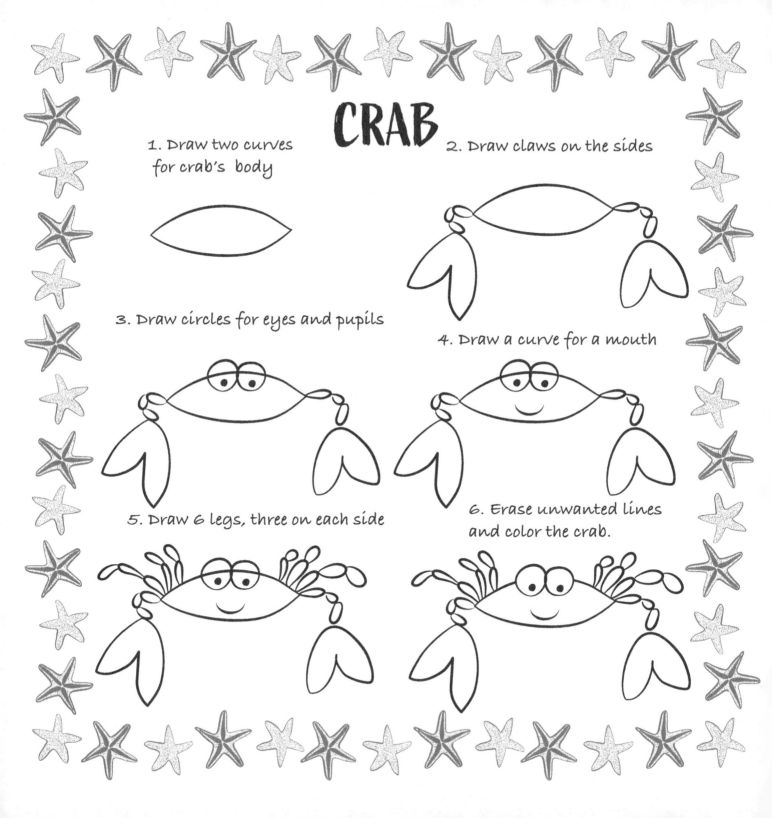

Now it is your turn!

Now it is your turn!

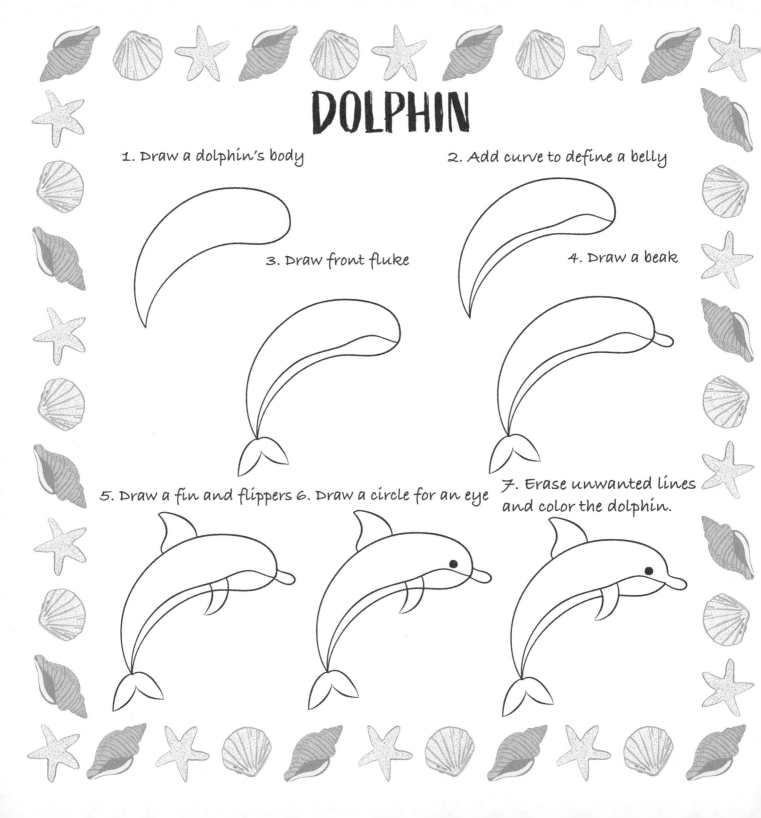

Now it is your turn!

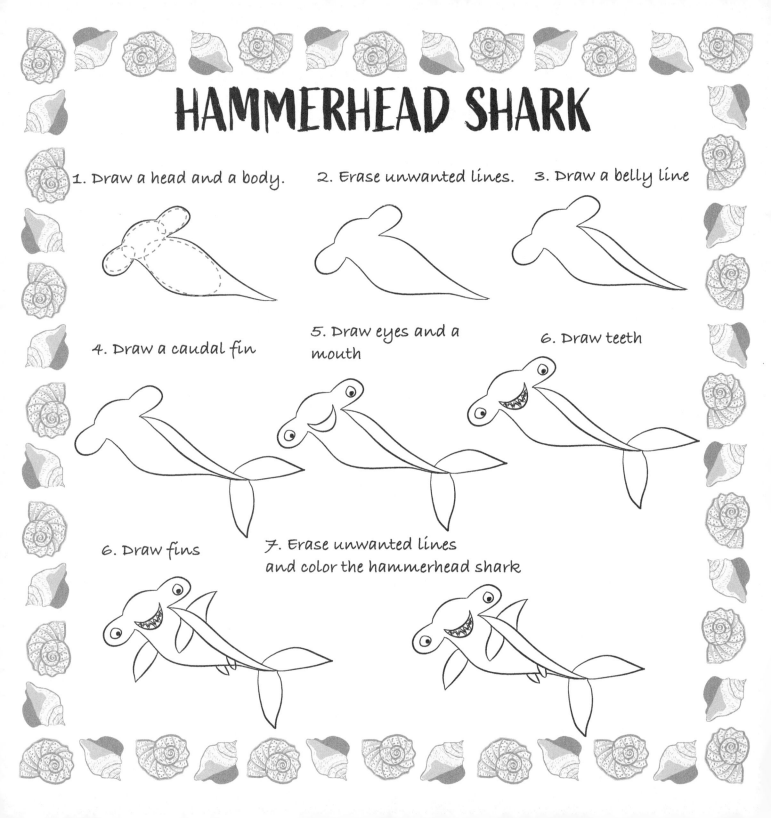

Now it is your turn!

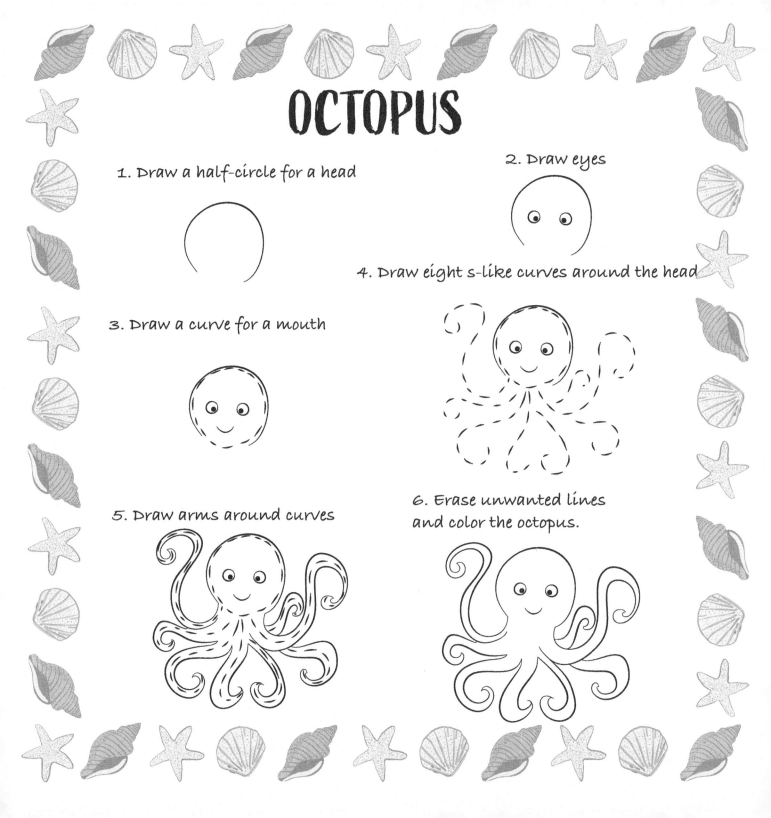

Did you enjoy drawing tutorials in this book?
Would you like more tutorials like this?
Join our newsletter and receive 5 Farm Animals Tutorials
free delivered to your mailbox.
Scan QR code with your smart phone now.

or visit www.smartkidpress.com/how-to-draw-farm-animals

www.smartkidpress.com

Made in the USA
Middletown, DE
13 April 2023